The girl who was sad

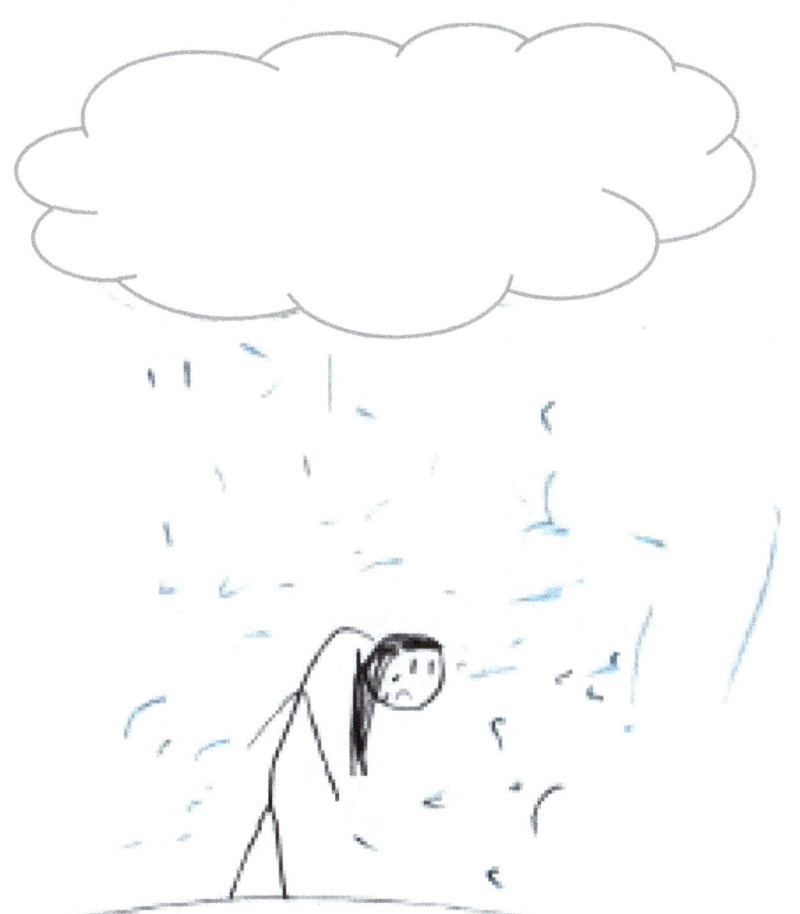

TO - Everyone who is feeling sad.

—Ember

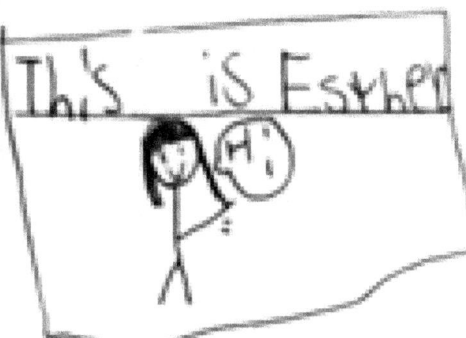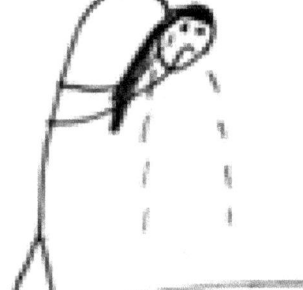

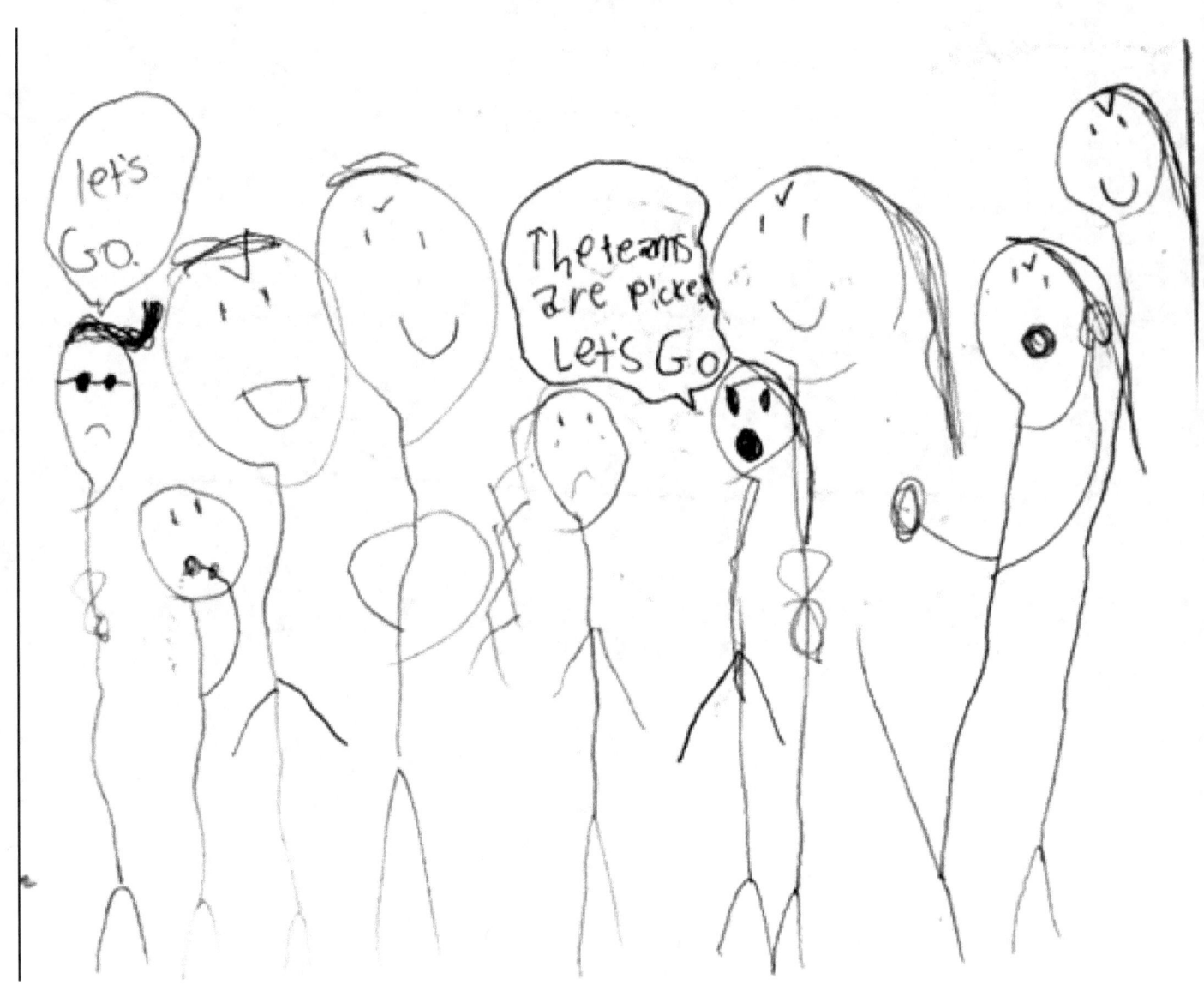

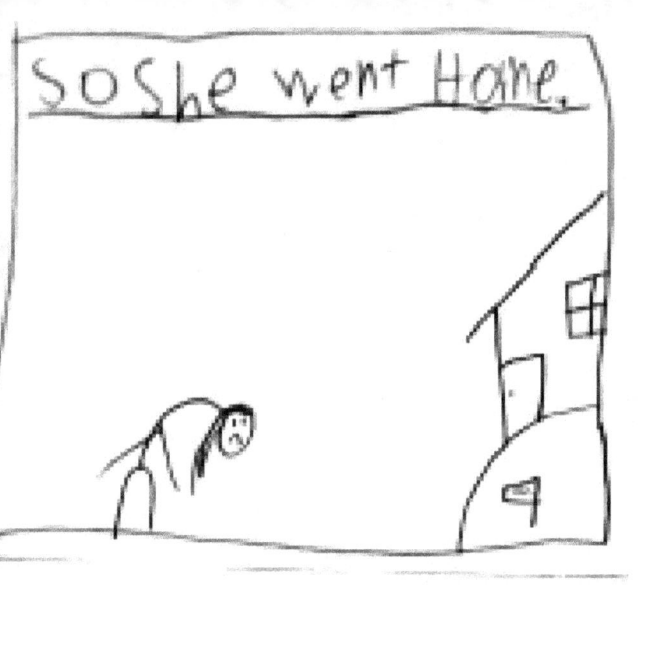
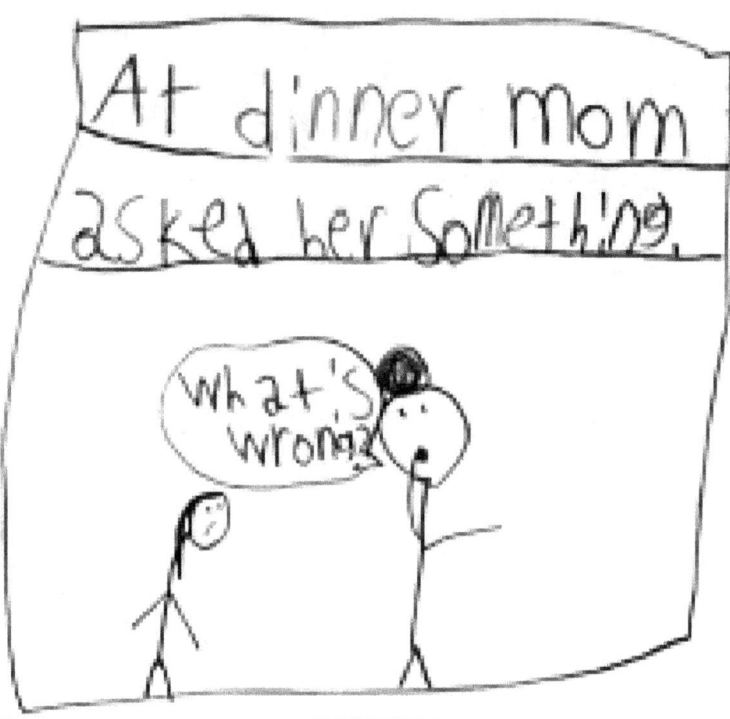
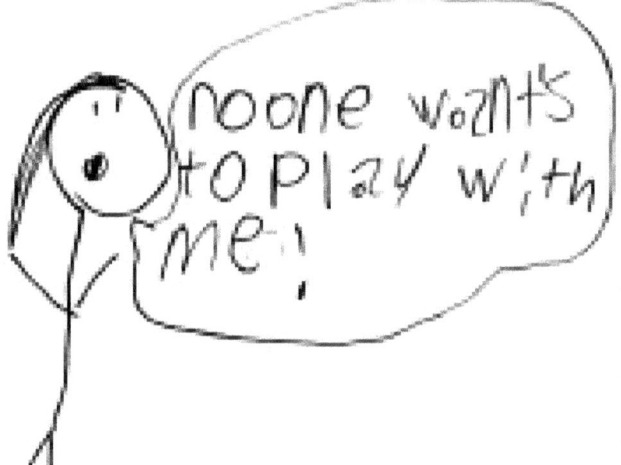
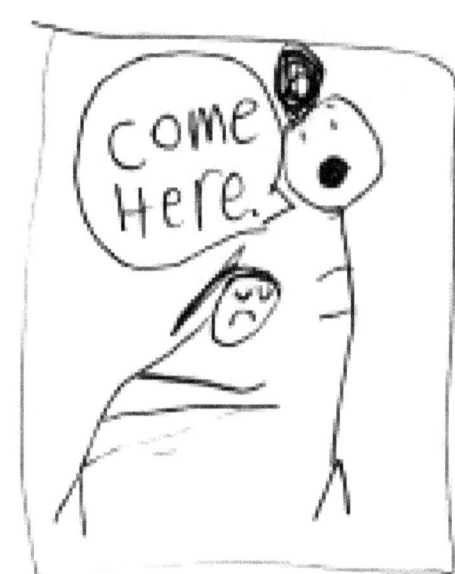
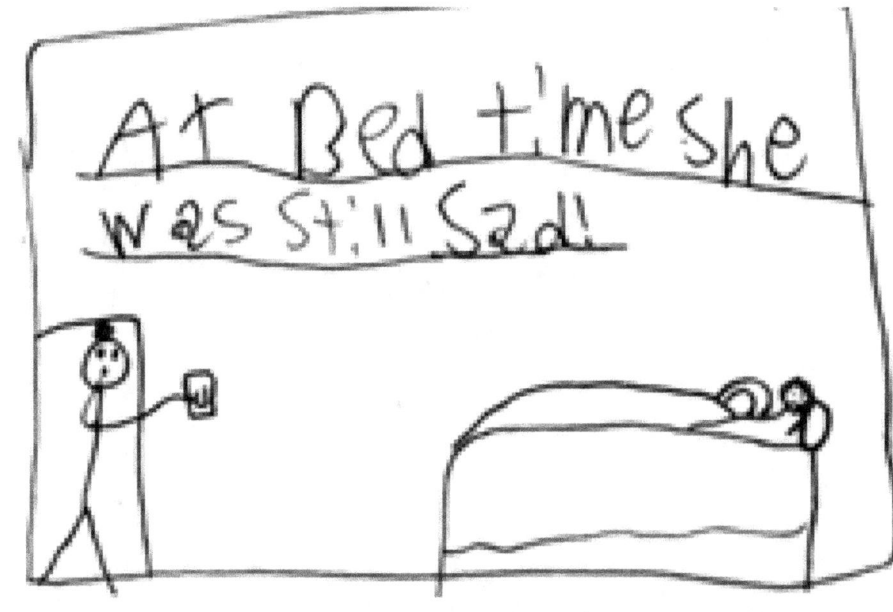

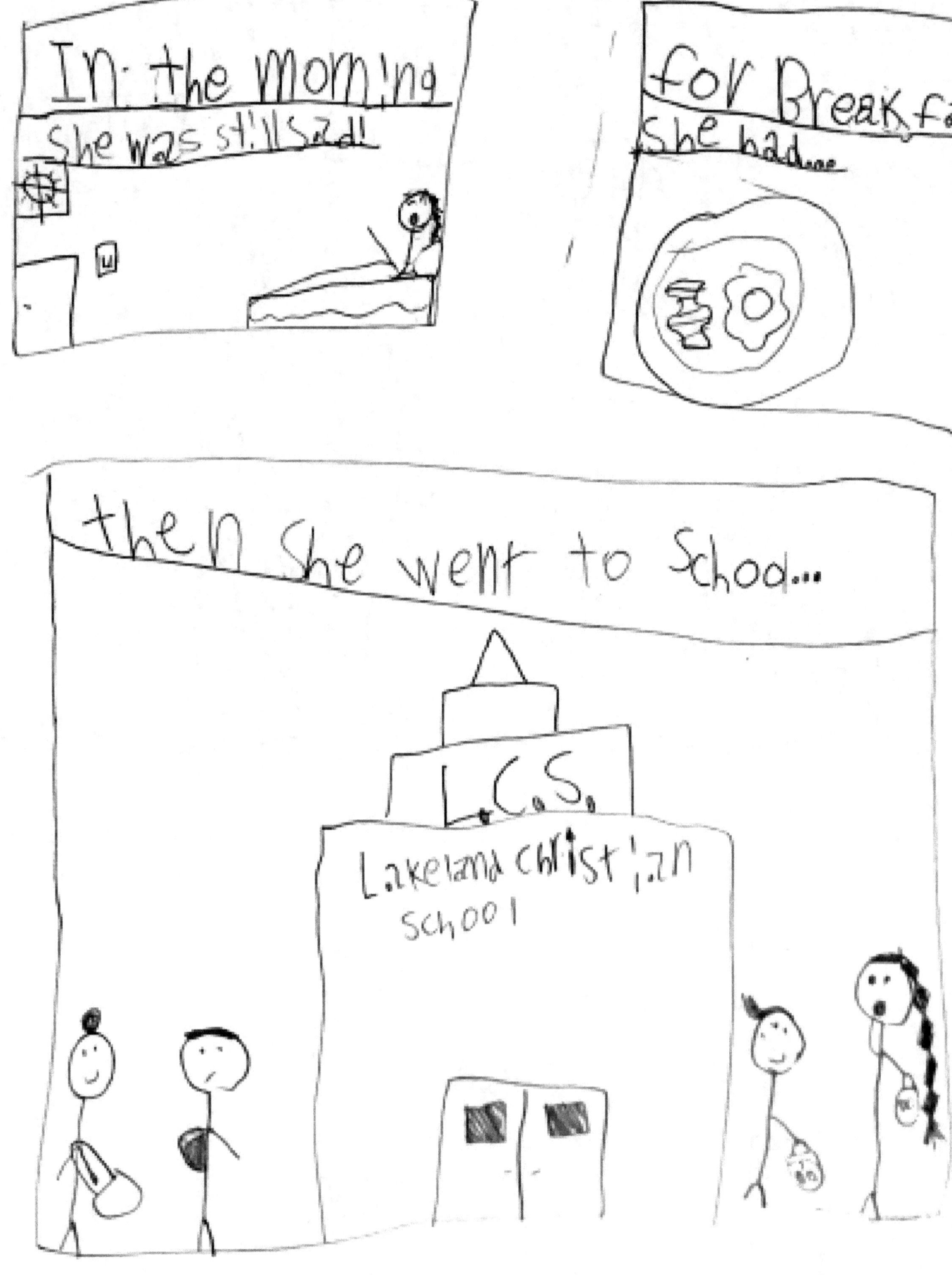

At recess

Hi!

And She was Happy!

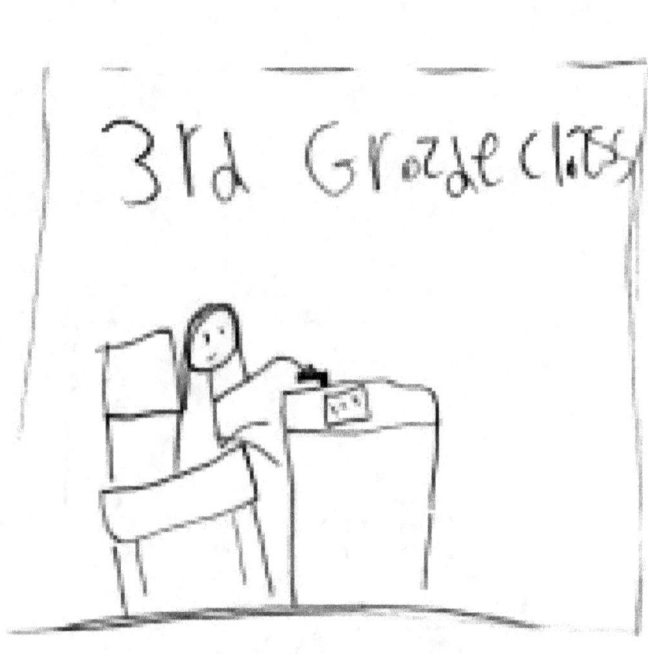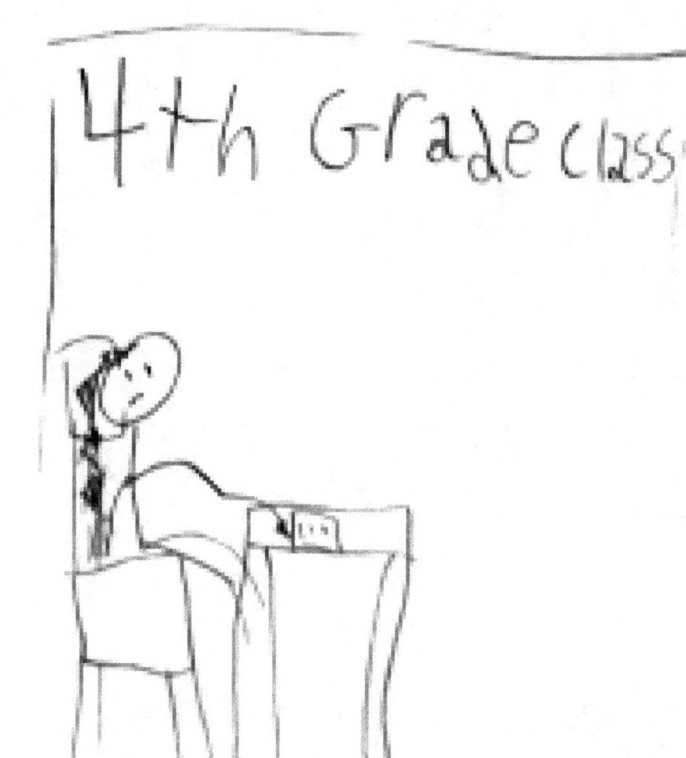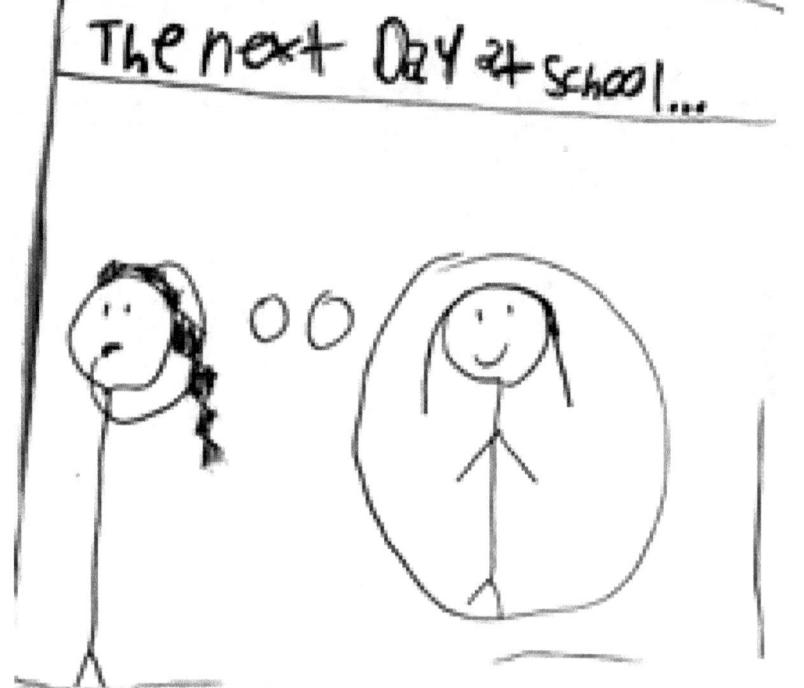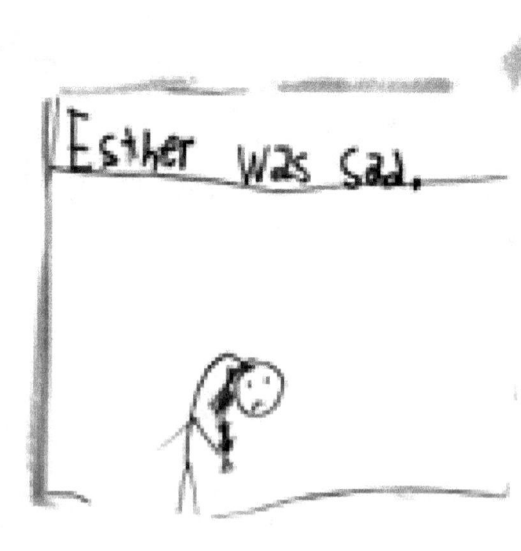

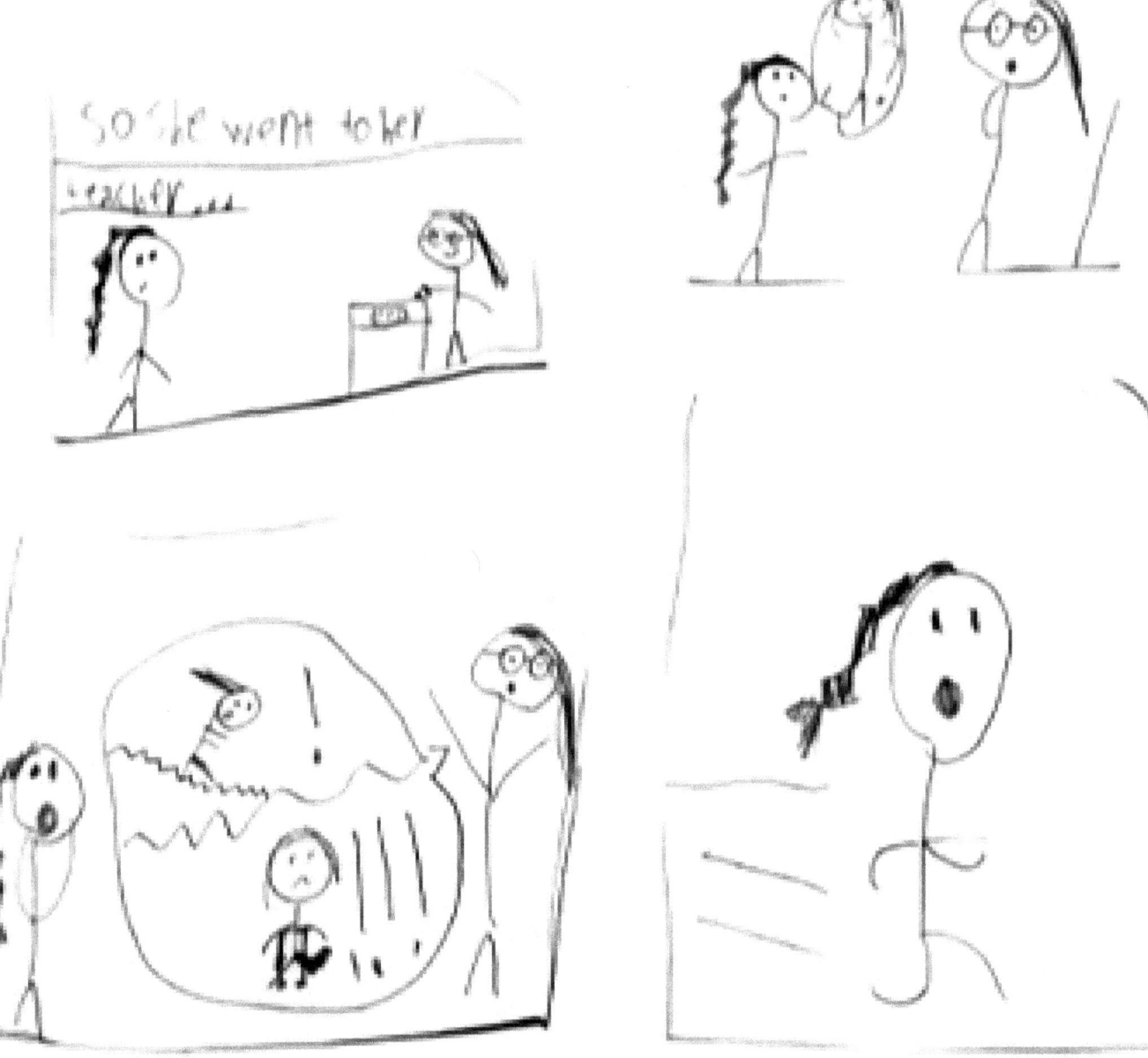

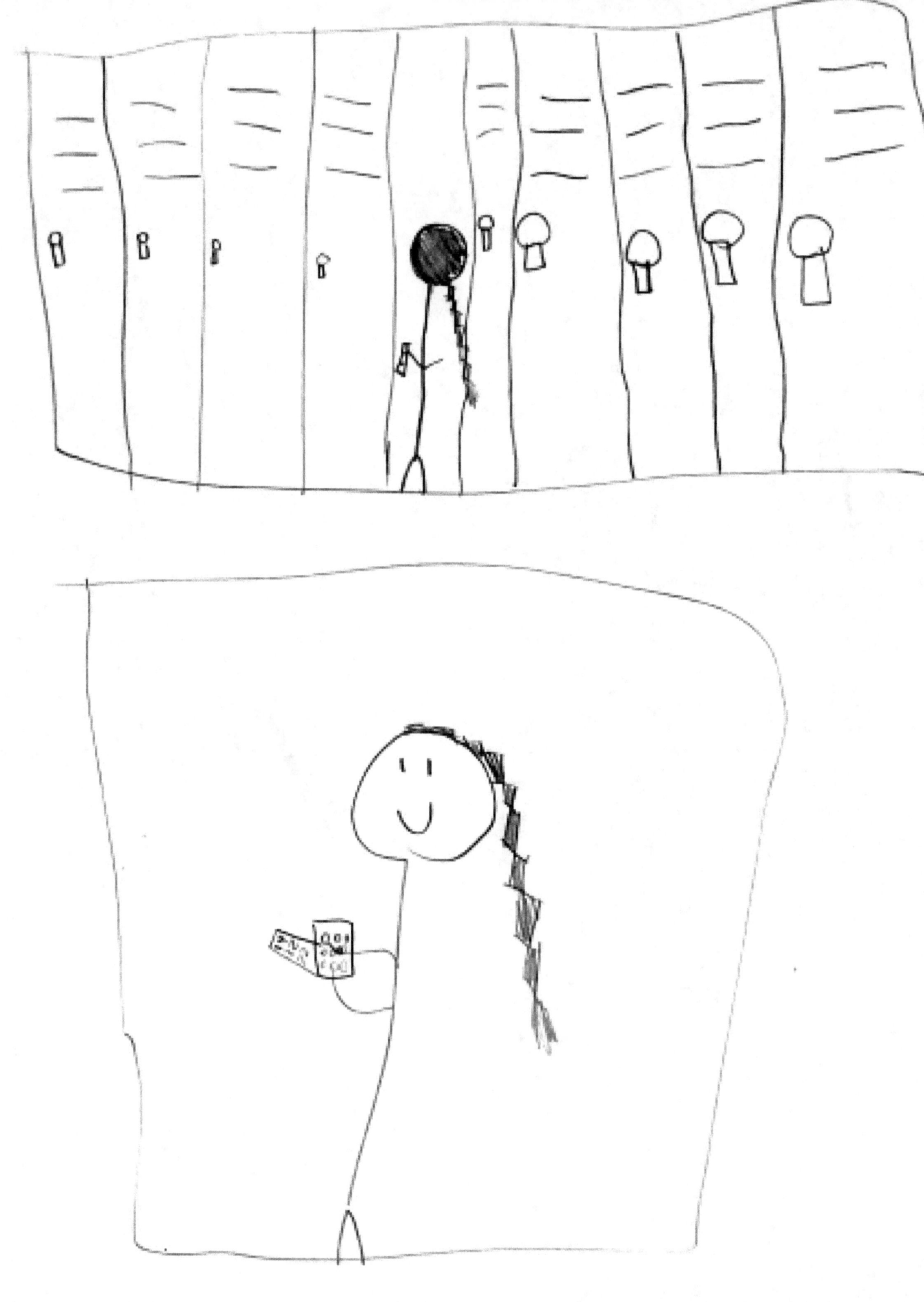

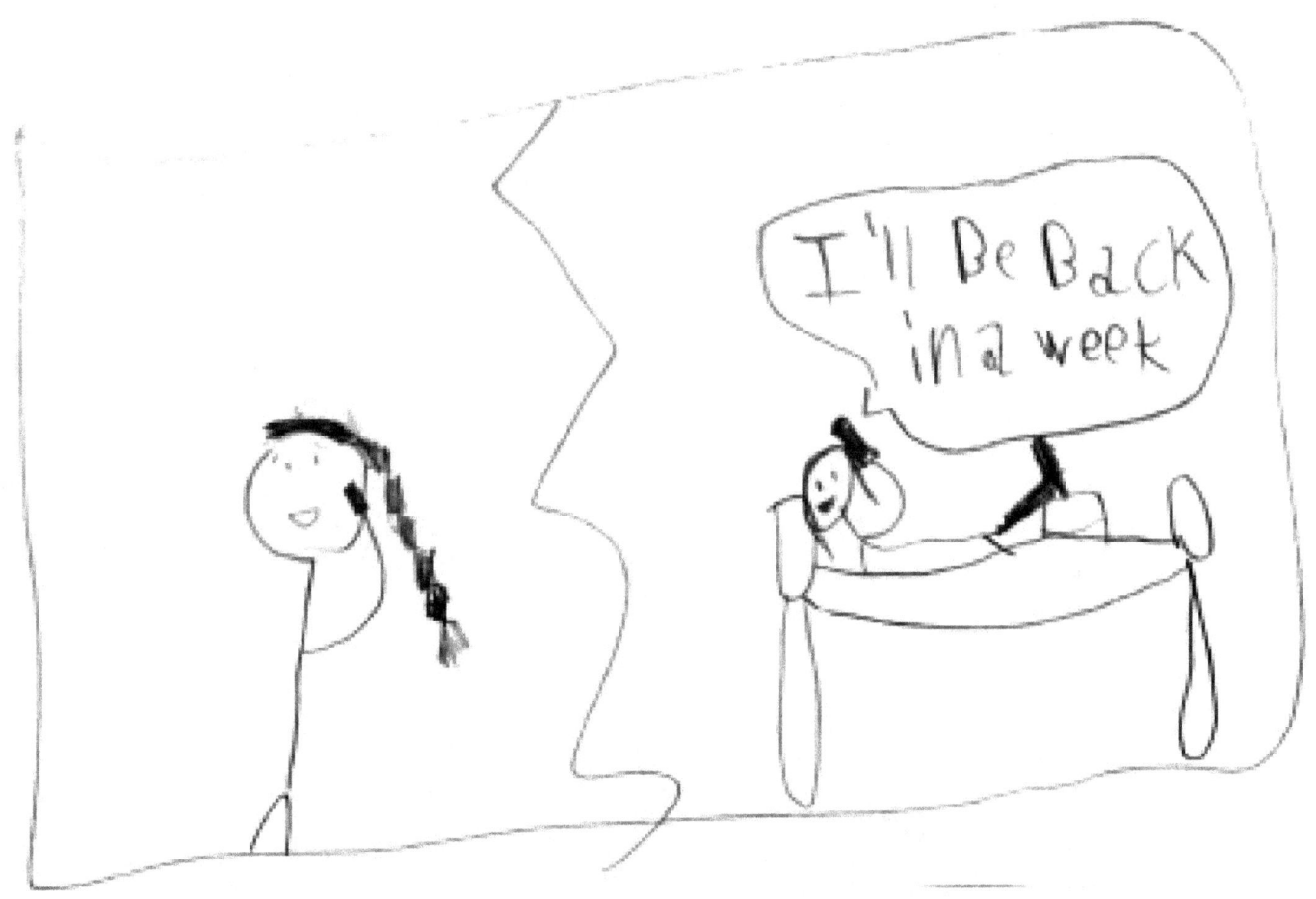

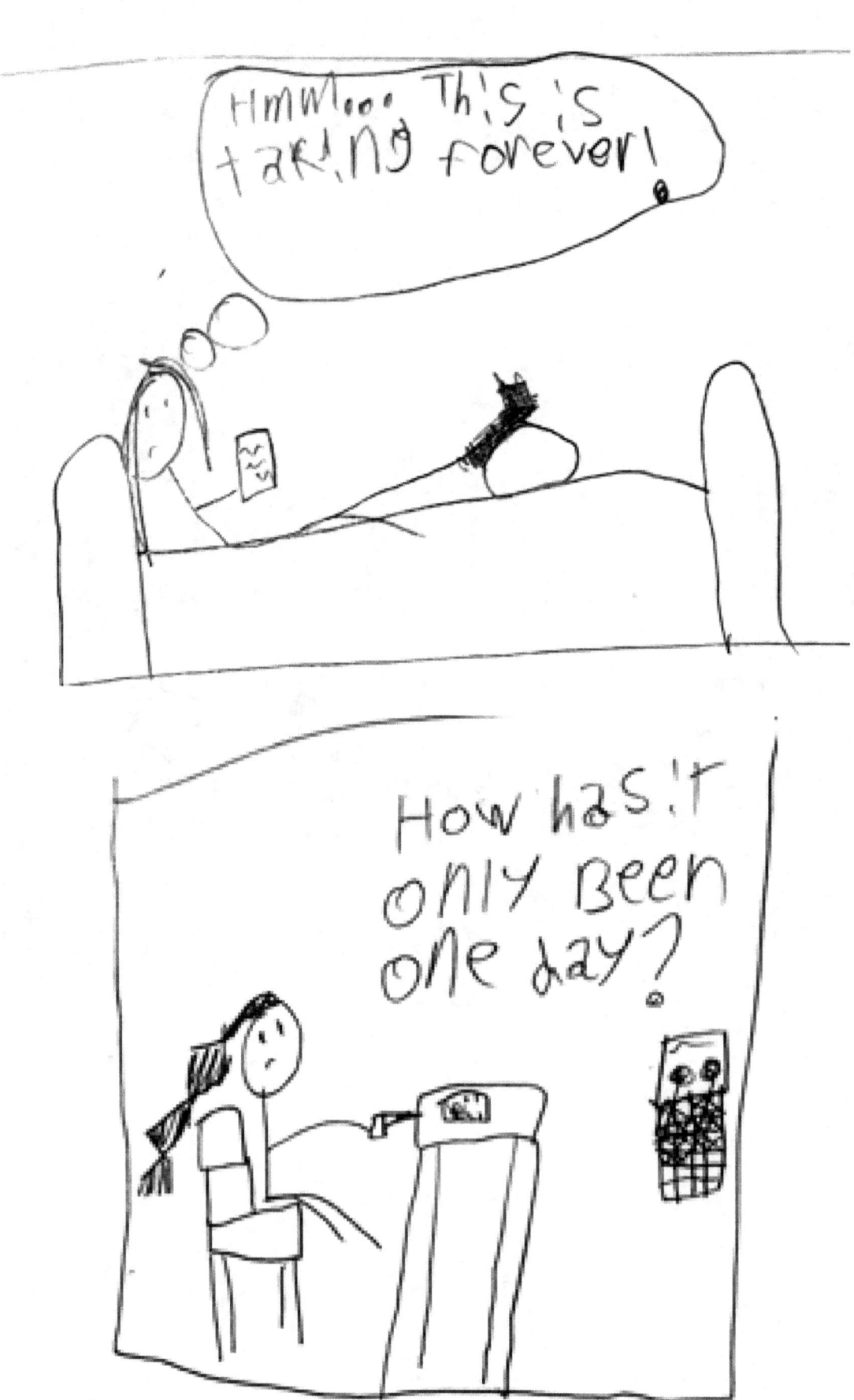

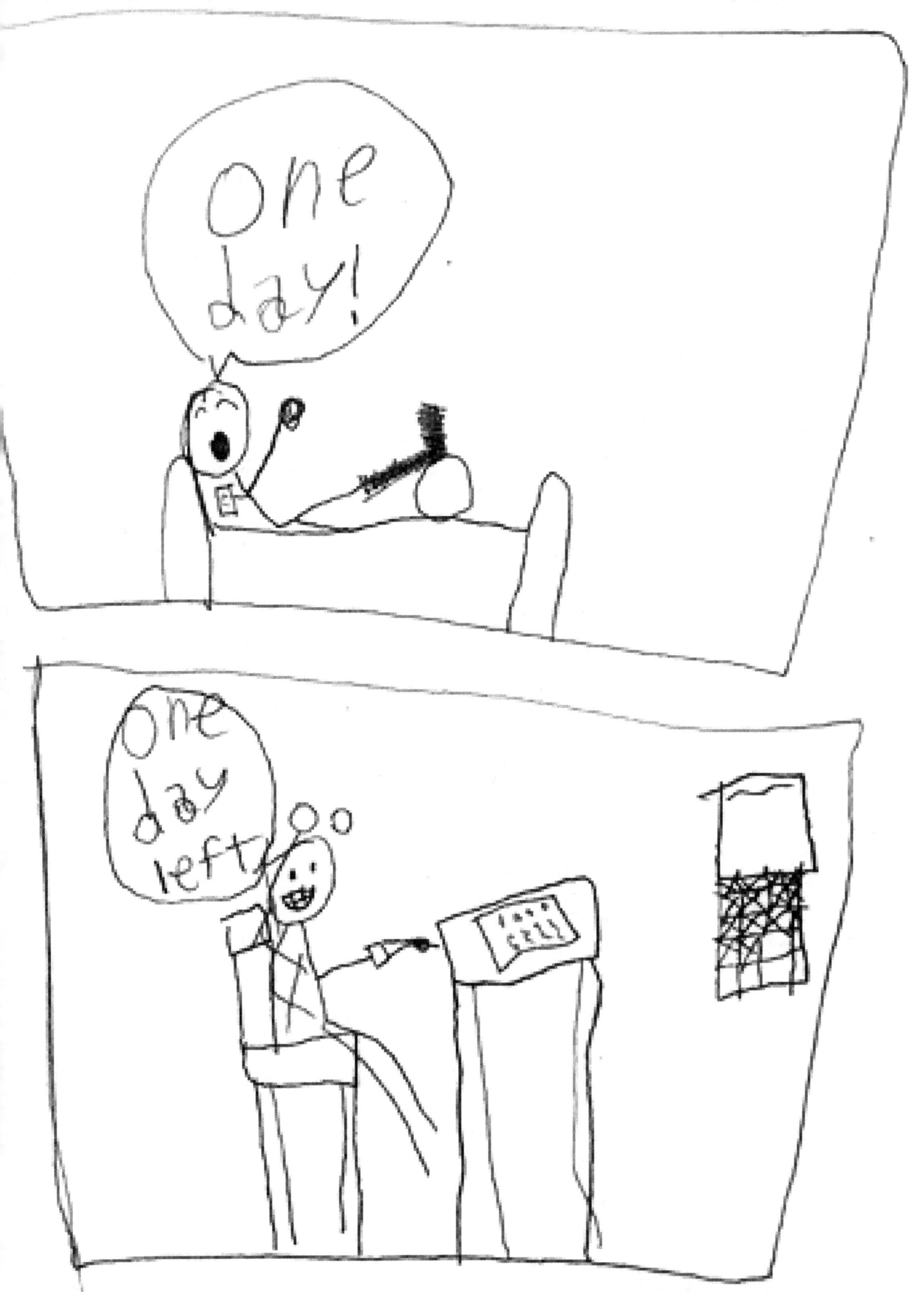

The next Day...

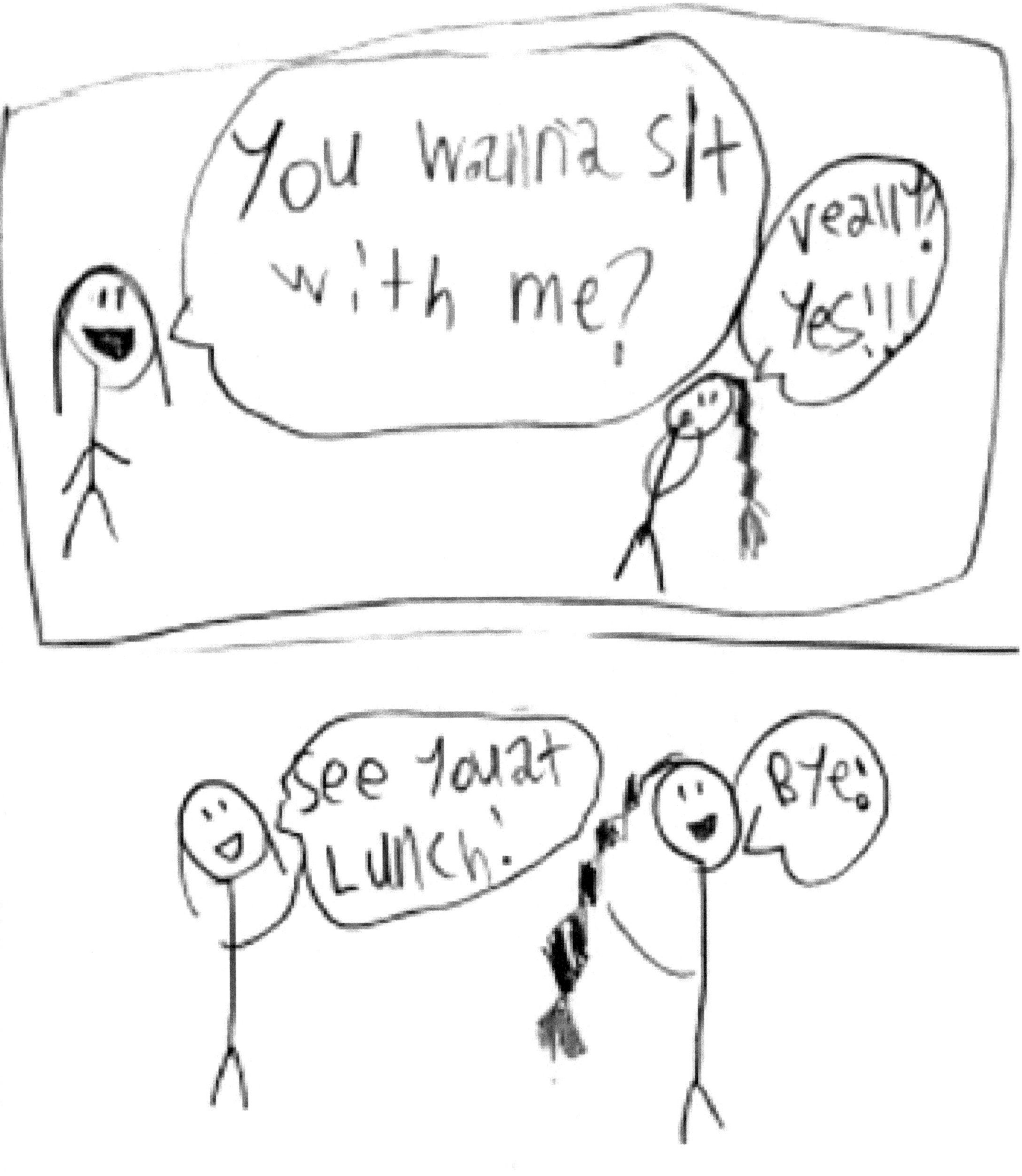

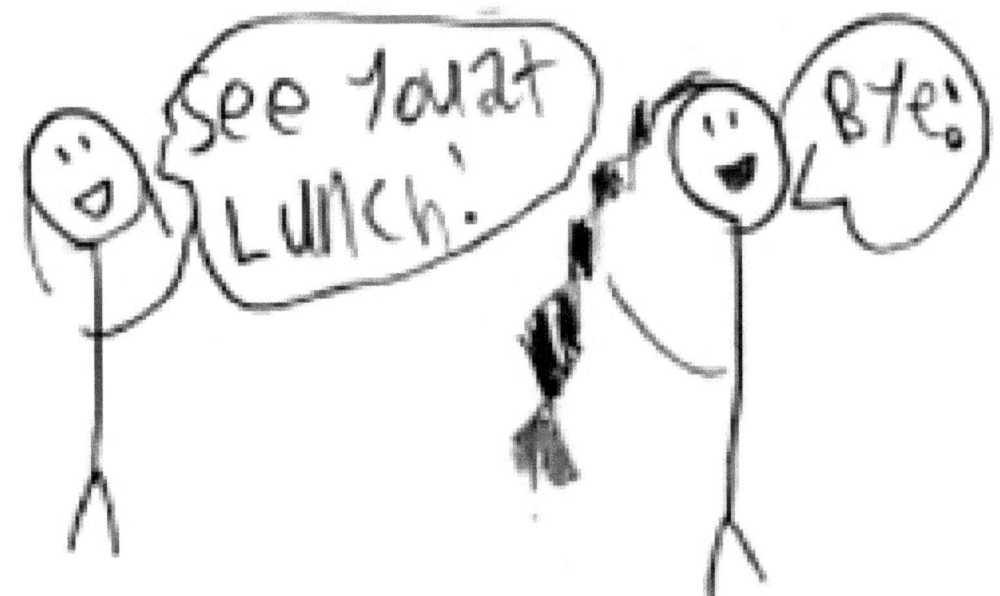

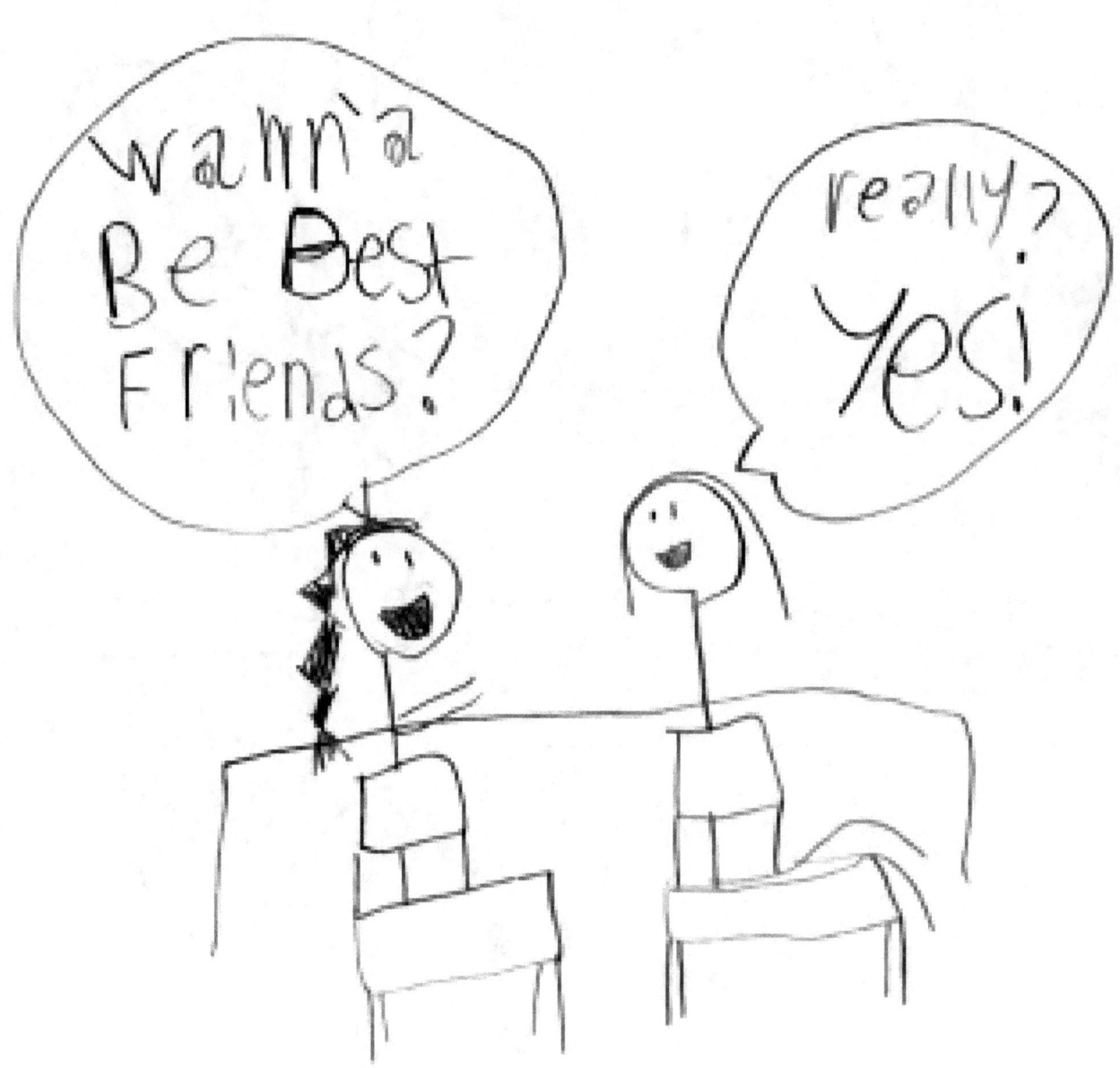

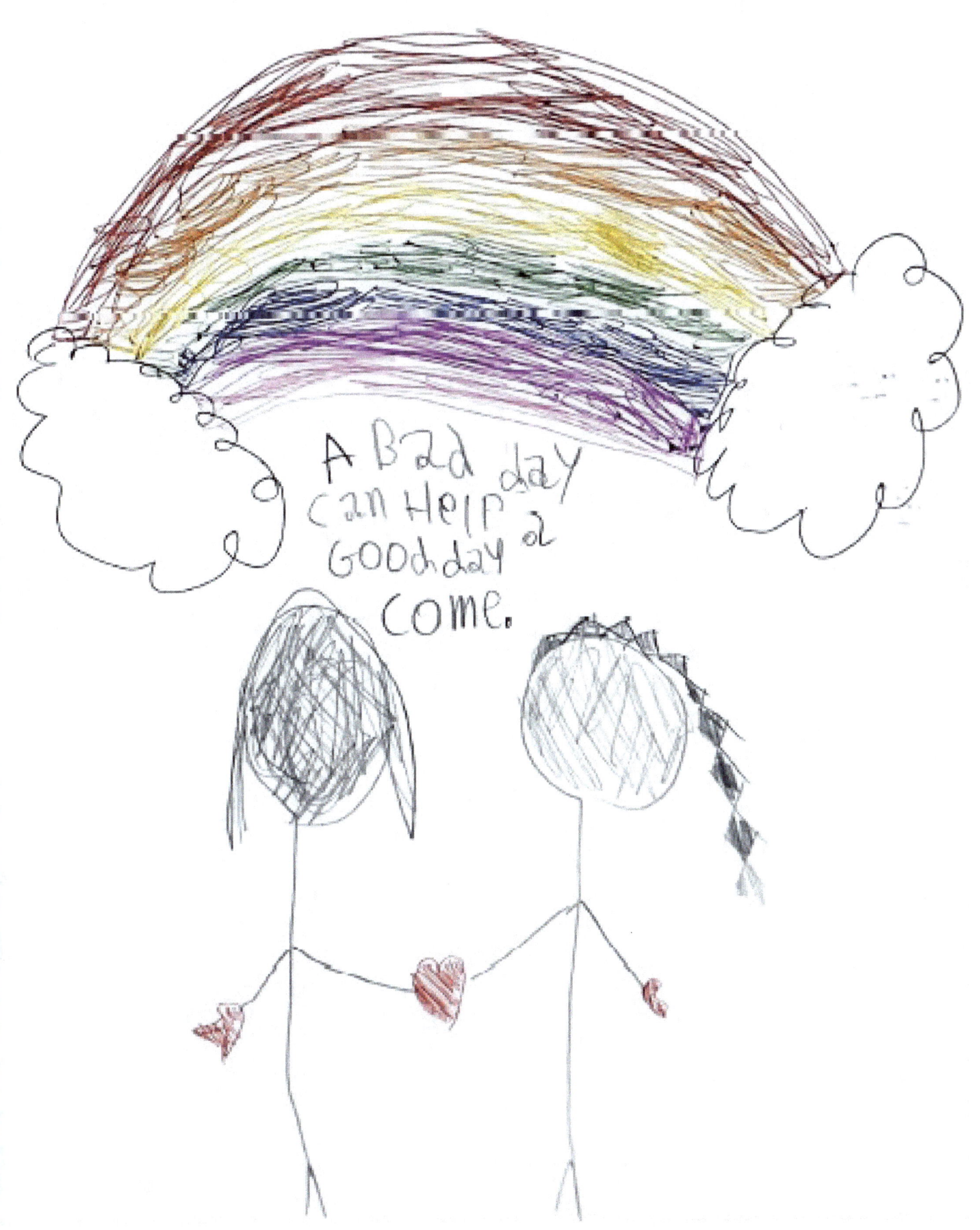

www.ingramcontent.com/pod-product-compliance
Lightning Source LLC
LaVergne TN
LVHW060134080526
838201LV00118B/3052